AMAZING JOHN

the story of John the XXIII, a charismatic pope
translated by Nancy Bels

AMAZING JOHN

BY DR. FRED LADENIUS

gift publications
Costa Mesa, CA 92626

*You bring me news of a door that opens at the end of a
corridor.
Sunlight and singing: when I had felt sure that every
corridor only led to another, or to a blank wall.*

            T. S. Eliot "The Family Reunion"

International Standard Book Number: 0-86595-008-3
Library of Congress Catalog Card Number: 81-86384
Gift Publications, Costa Mesa, CA 92626

*To
Giuseppe
Rosa*

Ten days before his death, he appears for the last time on the balcony, to greet the crowds.

AMAZING JOHN

INTRODUCTION

Pope John. Beloved John. There was a driving force, a secret in his life, and I believe every man, every woman should know this secret. So many people these past years have said to me: "You, you knew him, you were at the Vatican during his time, you followed the Council day after day as a journalist. Now you should write, tell us who he was, what he was like, why he was what he was — how he could be what he was and yet remain what he was!"

Many books, articles, and essays have been written about him; it is not my intention here to do another hagiography in the manner of "Lives of the Saints." Certainly, John was a saint, a saint of God sanctified in Jesus Christ. But unctuous religiosity was far from him — the religiosity of the so-called "born holy" was to drive many away from the faith.

To his own, to the church, John wanted to teach that conversion is the awakening of a new self; the vital element in the new birth is the dawning of a new affection. Conversion is, in fact, a falling in love, a saying "yes" to the Divine Love. And it is this passion for the Unseen, the Eternal, which above all else can change the heart, strengthen the will, and illuminate the mind: this is the birth of love. John was in love with Love, and like all lovers he spoke about his Love "in season and out of season". He had lived, experienced an inner transformation, operated

9

by love, and since then he had lived in faith: faith as a fruit of, a result of, the experience. Faith, in fact, begins when the God outwardly professed is inwardly experienced. "God-outside-of-us" is a theory; God inside of us is a fact. God outside of us is hypothesis; God inside of us an experience. God the Father is the possibility of salvation, God the Spirit is the actualization: of life, of joy, of peace, of saving and healing power. To his own, to the church, by his effect more than by his words, John was able to convey his experience. He would have liked working as part of a team but was obliged to do many things alone, humanly speaking, only relying on his Divine Helper. Opposed, misunderstood, he was able to say things that, said before his time and by anyone other than John, would have been condemned by the Catholic Church.

He spoke as a free man in order to free us in truth and in love. He would have liked to have a team, we have said, but he had to fight alone for the unity he so desired. To us all, he taught the difference between the little things we can do alone, and the big things we can do together. With some pain and much joy we are discovering the fascination and power of a God-controlled team.

Thank you, beloved John. You prayed to receive gifts we weren't capable of understanding when you asked the Lord for the gift of a new Pentecost in your church.

"The effective prayer of a righteous man can accomplish much." (James 5 : 16).

You were a righteous man, John, and God is faithful to keep His promise.

FRED LADENIUS

There came a man, sent from God, whose name was John.

He came for a witness, that he might bear witness of the light, that all might believe through him.

He was not the light, but *came* that he might bear witness of the light.

John 1:6-8

1. A BRIDGE NEEDED

Slowly, a drop of blood ran down his cheek. That morning while shaving, Angelo Roncalli had cut himself. It was something that rarely happened, since at his age everything had to be done methodically, with precision. There were the wrinkles, that double chin, making the job even more difficult. It has to be done...it has to be done. That is easy to say; sometimes, just when age is advancing but the spirit has stayed young, a desire for haste surges up, a desire to do everything possible in the short time left.

Pope Pius had just died. Angelo had left Venice, where he was bishop, to come to Rome for the election of the new Pope. He had come to elect, not to be elected.

At the Vatican, the room Angelo was staying in was dark and somber. The chipped mirror reflecting his image — old, but not antique — must have been the same age he was: 78.

Outside, the sun shone brilliantly. The sky was clear, high, and the hills of Albano seemed within hand's reach. The weather, as it often did on an October day in Rome, was signaling the end of a long summer. Angelo thought about Venice, about the pile of correspondence growing daily on his desk. He loved Venice, and especially the Venetians, who were of the same breed as himself. Of course, Venice was a very humid city; he could feel it in his bones. The Roman sun would have been a balm for his aches. In Rome he could have taken walks, sat on a bench, and enjoyed the warmth of the early afternoon hours, from Christmas to Easter. For several years, first in Paris, where he had been the papal ambassador, and then in Venice, where the people called him "patriarch", he had the impression that the winters were becoming longer and colder. In Rome the winters were short, lukewarm, mere interludes between one summer and another. Angelo knew her well, Rome: he had spent three years there in seminary, after the five years of study at Bergamo, from 1896 to 1901. He returned there once again after that, to the office of "Propaganda Fide" from 1921 to 1924. It would be wonderful to return for a third time, to stay forever. But for Angelo, to return would mean to become Pope, at the age of seventy-eight.

Angelo looked at himself in the mirror and saw the blood continue to flow. Seventy-eight years old. Quite a lot for a mirror which was not of the first quality. Quite a lot for a man — even one of solid peasant stock. His election would be absurd.

Pius XII was an octogenarian when he died, and for years at the Vatican they had whispered that the old Pontiff was **really** getting old. No, you don't elect a man of seventy-eight years to lead a church of over 600 million souls. Unless...unless you elect him **because** of his age. After the long pontificate of Pius XII, someone had suggested the necessity of a "transitory pontificate", of a "business government" as they say in politics, of a Pope who would name new cardinals — now that the number of these was reduced from seventy to fifty-four — and who would serve as a "bridge" from the late Pope until the election of a new one.

The conclave, meeting of the Roman Catholic cardinals called to elect a new Pope, had begun on October 25, 1958.

That morning the fifty-two cardinals who were in Rome assisted at a Votive Mass of the Holy Ghost, in St. Peter's, and listened to an exhortation given by Monsignor Antonio Bacci: "We have need of a pontiff with great strength of mind and ardent charity, a pontiff who knows how to tell the truth even to those who do not wish to hear it, who knows how to defend the rights of Christian and human civilization, but at the same time opening arms of pardon to all, even to those who make bloody the heart of our common Father... he must be a teacher... and a pastor... and also himself a father."

"May he be like a bridge between heaven and earth, may he be like a bridge between social classes. Finally, may he be like a bridge between nations, even among those who reject, repel, and persecute the Christian religion. Above all, there is need of a holy Pope, because a holy Pope may obtain things from God which natural gifts cannot provide."

Angelo meditated each word of that speech, one after another. A bridge, a bridge, a bridge. Between heaven and earth. Between social classes. Between nations. And who was capable of being that bridge? There had been, gathered around that altar, fifty-two cardinals, several of whom could be considered *papabili* — eligible for the papacy.

In the speculations of the press, the conservative *papabili* were the Italian cardinals Ottaviani, Maselli, and Ruffini. The liberal leader was the Italian cardinal Lercaro.

For the first time in four centuries several non-Italians were considered to have a very good chance of election. Cardinal Agagianian, a liberal, was first on the list. Another was Cardinal Tisserant, whose wisdom and long experience as a world traveler made him an eligible candidate. Some newspapers publicized the chances of Francis Spelman, the Cardinal Archbishop of New York, a brilliant conservative.

The future of the church, as a human organization, seemed uncertain. That morning Angelo had written to a dear friend, Giuseppe Piazzi, bishop of Bergamo: "My soul is comforted with confidence in the new Pentecost which will enable us to give a new vigor to the victory of truth, to what is good, and to peace through the renewal of the Head of the Holy Church...". A new Pentecost. For some time this idea had come to him, each time he retired for prayer. Why "Pentecost"? If there was one celebration which, more than any other, had lost its meaning, its sense, it was certainly that of Pentecost, the harvest of the fiftieth day. It had been on the day of Pentecost that, according to the book of Acts, the outpouring of the Holy Spirit took place, upon the disciples gathered together in Jerusalem. There, since the day of Jesus' ascension, they had been praying and awaiting the accomplishment of His promise. Pentecost was the divine response to the Tower of Babel. The Tower symbolized unity coming from below, human pride seeking to lift itself up to heaven and ending only in chaos. The unity of the church, in contrast, cannot be manufactured, it is received and manifested through faith.

The Holy Spirit falls at Pentecost and makes of a little group of disciples a community committed to evangelizing the world, to announcing the Word of God.

16

Pentecost. Angelo would speak about Pentecost to Rome and to the world, once elected. About Pentecost and about the Holy Spirit. In the Catholic Church, He had for years been the forgotten One, and Angelo knew this.

In the days of his next-to-last Pentecost on earth, Sunday June 10, 1962, he was to address a prayer to God and a message to the world, known to history as "Pope John's prayer to the Holy Spirit".

"To the Holy Spirit, Paraclete, perfect the work begun in us by Jesus. Strengthen and continue our prayer on behalf of the entire world. Bring forth for each one of us a time of deep interior life; give vigor to our apostleship, our desire to reach all men and all peoples. All saved by the blood of Christ and all part of His heritage. Put to death that natural presumptuousness and lift us into the regions of holy humility, of the true fear of God, of generous courage... may all be larger in us: the seeking after truth, the readiness to sacrifice even to the cross and death. And may all, finally, be in accord with the last prayer of the Son to the Heavenly Father, and this baptism of You, O Holy Spirit of Love, the Father and the Son grant it to the Church and to each of her institutions, to each soul and to all peoples." Amen, amen, hallelujah, hallelujah!"

But let us return to that October 25, 1958. In Rome, outdoors, the sun was still shining. The sky was still clear and the hills of Albano seemed to come even closer, to be even more within arms' reach.

A drop, another drop, and yet another drop of blood streaked the cheek of the old man with the wonderfully young heart.

Four days after his election as Pope, he would surprise everyone by announcing the new name he had chosen for himself: "I will be called John."

Why John? Already the cardinals were thinking of the Baptist, or the Evangelist — John the Beloved — when Angelo explained the reason for his choice: "John is my father's name." Later, he would confide to a friend, "I chose the name also because I wanted a name that would be not only Catholic, but also Christian."

John XXIII signs the encyclical letter "PACEM IN TERRIS" —
Peace on earth. April 9, 1963.

Whereas you have been forsaken and hated
With no one passing through,
I will make you an everlasting pride,
A joy from generation to generation.
You will also suck the milk of nations,
And will suck the breast of kings;
Then you will know that I, the Lord, am your Saviour,
And your Redeemer, the mighty One of Jacob.

Isaiah 60:15-16

2. KNOW-SO SALVATION

Thus was born Pope John. Within the thick Vatican walls, John would be, from the beginning to the end of his pontificate, a man alone. Alone with God! There would be no clan around him, no "Roncallian party", no priestly mafia. His *confrères* and friends are humble, modest people who live lives of sacrifice and prayer. Men of God who haven't made a "career" in the Church. They are scattered, his friends; they live in little mountain parishes, or far away beyond the sea, on mission fields, there where people pray and work for the coming of the Kingdom of God.

John had also prayed and worked in faraway countries. Several years earlier, in Bulgaria, where he was representing the Vatican, John had written: "Being aware of the difference between my way of seeing things and certain Roman points of view causes me great pain. This is my real cross."

However, despite the preoccupations and misunderstandings, John always lived in serenity and joy. Without a doubt this was because in his heart dwelt a certainty that is rare among us, believers of the Roman Catholic Church: the certainty of salvation. John knew that the blood of Jesus Christ washed away all his sins. I know many practicing Catholics who would never dare affirm with any assurance that their ultimate destination was

21

heaven. John was certain. John was one of those who take the word of God seriously. "Whosoever shall call on the name of the Lord Jesus shall be saved." Words leaving no place for doubt. They were words he had hidden in his heart and mind, like precious treasure. Like these verses of Psalm 23, his favorite: "The Lord is my shepherd, I shall not want. He maketh me to lie down in green pastures; He leadeth me beside the still waters. He restoreth my soul; He leadeth me in the paths of righteousness for His name's sake. Yea, though I walk through the valley of the shadow of death I will fear no evil, for thou art with me, thy rod and thy staff they comfort me. Thou preparest a table before me in the presence of mine enemies; thou anointest my head with oil, my cup runneth over. Surely goodness and mercy shall follow me all the days of my life, and I will dwell in the house of the Lord forever."

In this psalm of David, John discovered, in all its splendor and depth, the eternal truth of the personal relationship between man and his personal Savior, Jesus Christ. Christ, the Savior of all humanity, of all those who through the centuries would accept the free gift of His sacrifice; and, at the same time, the personal Savior of every man and every woman who, like Peter, would be willing to recognize in Him the living God.

Assurance and humility were the leitmotifs of his existence. In the first chapter of the Gospel of John, we read that a man came, a man sent from God, and that his name was John. "He came as a witness, that he might bear witness of the light, that all might believe through him." I believe that these words could also be applied to Pope John. If the Baptist was the herald of the first coming of the true light, then John was the herald of the

New Pentecost for the Roman Catholic Church, of the great outpouring of the Spirit of God, prelude to the second coming of Christ. Like the Baptist, Pope John was the forerunner, the harbinger of the wonders of our time. But in the plan of God it was already written that he himself would not know them.

In his Gospel, chapter 3, verses 29-30, the Evangelist brings us these words of John the Baptist: "He who has the bride is the bridegroom. But the friend of the bridegroom, who stands and hears him, rejoices greatly because of the bridegroom's voice..."

John XXIII, friend of the bridegroom, friend of Jesus. Concerned about the destiny of the bride, desiring to see her "glorious, without spot or wrinkle or any such thing, but... holy and blameless." (Ephesians 5:27). Once again a man came, and his name was John. He admired Peter's sincere humility, and often cited the episode reported in the book of Acts concerning Peter's visit to Cesarea. Luke tells how Peter set off and arrived in Cesarea the next day. Cornelius was waiting for him there, having invited close friends and relatives. As Peter was about to enter, Cornelius went to meet him, and threw himself down to worship Peter. But Peter lifted him up, saying, "I, too, am a man."

Shepherd of the largest of the Christian churches, John knew that the Lord was *his* Shepherd, the Pastor of all the sheep. Three times Jesus had asked Simon Peter if he loved Him, and three times to his affirmative answer, the Lord had said "Feed my sheep." *My* sheep. The Lord's sheep. The sheep of the Good Shepherd. John's Shepherd. The Shepherd who encouraged and guided him in the paths of righteousness for His name's sake.

23

Yes, John had the certainty of salvation. This is why he could say, "He who has faith will never tremble. Death is a momentary separation. We should all be able to gather together for ever, there where we will be better off than here, where we can enjoy eternity. I have no fear of death; I see ancestors and friends who have preceded me there, waiting to joyfully welcome me and lead me to the Father. No, I have no fear of the hereafter beyond these walls; I *see* the heavenly gallery."

He did not say, "I hope so"; he did not say, "if God wills it...''; he did not say, "maybe one day we will see each other in heaven". John knew that God keeps all His promises. He knew that everything was paid by Christ on the cross at Golgotha. That we must only believe, accept, praise the Giver of all gifts. Not only the gift of salvation: is it not written that if we, who are evil, know how to give good gifts to our children, how much more will the Heavenly Father give the Holy Spirit to those who ask Him? Ask. Not those who deserve it or who pay the price to obtain it. Like all gifts, the Holy Spirit is a free gift. And it was the Holy Spirit that John's church urgently needed.

In a church where the Holy Spirit is loved and called upon, the gifts of the Spirit bloom — while structures and institutions take on their proper perspective — as the Spirit blows through like a fresh wind of liberty.

It was the Spirit of God making John speak as no one had spoken in Rome since Peter and Paul. The entire world was listening. He spoke of union, of ecumenism, of reciprocal fault. Many Christians, who had long since stopped hoping for anything from Rome, were surprised and at the same time deeply touched by this unexpected manner of speaking. John said, "We will not try to determine who was right and who was wrong — is the blame to fall on our separated brothers? In part, but a large part of the blame is ours." "Let us place value on those things which unite us, and lay aside that which separates." "To enter into God's realm of judgement is a dangerous thing, and all too often we have judged." "Christianity", said John at Easter, 1959, "is not a grouping together of oppressing laws, as so often is said by those who have no faith: Christianity is peace and joy and love, and life ever renewing itself, like the secret pulse-beat of nature at springtime."

Henceforth, the reformers know that the Pope is on their side, without hesitation... For twenty minutes John would speak of the council, of "his" council, as the Spirit of God showed him. A fraternal gathering in sign of a newfound freedom.

In Rome the "Council Fathers" begin to arrive, coming from the four corners of the earth. And with them come the brothers in Jesus Christ. These are the Armenian Orthodox, the Egyptians, the Syrians, the Russians, the Lutherans and the Baptists, Episcopalians, Quakers, Old Catholics, Congregationalists.

Each time we confess a belief in the Holy Spirit, we proclaim at the same time our faith in a living God, able and desiring to intervene in each human life and each situation, able to make all things new. And without the Holy Spirit in our personal lives, as well as in the life of the church as a community, there is neither conviction, nor sanctification, nor any work acceptable to the Lord.

In the life of every man there are milestones along the

way, and there were also some in the life of the man John. A milestone among milestones was certainly the spiritual retreat in Roustchouk, on the Black Sea, during the month of August, 1934, when he represented Pope Pius XI in Bulgaria. During that retreat John spent much time meditating the writings of Father Alphonse Gratry. We can say that between these two chosen souls there was a real "encounter". Father Alphonse Gratry (1805-1872) was a man of many talents. At once a man of the church, a scholar, a philosopher. In John's notes we discover certain of Father Gratry's thoughts.

To those who followed him, Father Gratry proposed a lofty goal: "The world you want to change into a just place will not be changed, because you yourselves have not been changed. The world will change if you are changed... I know that you, me, each one of us can add our actions, our weight, to the weight of sin moving us toward the abyss; or in the name of God and in union with Christ we can work to save the world and turn it around, to change the direction of this century and of history." It was first to the young people that Gratry addressed his message. In 1858, when the Communist Manifesto was already being spread throughout the world, this contemporary of Karl Marx wrote: "There is a new principle of heroism and enthusiasm with which God would like to inspire our generation. Let us open our hearts and our minds to this inspiration and this force. Isn't it time to begin the big changes, the true revolution, to introduce the nations to God's laws? We are able to control matter by applying known laws, to control ourselves and our behavior. When we return to the ancient wisdom, the greatest of all revolutions will take place. At that time, the Gospel prayer will be realized: 'Thy kingdom come, thy will be done, on earth as it is heaven'."

John with his secretary of state, Amleto Cicognani.
— "Why did you choose such an old man to be your secretary of state?"
— "He's not at all old; he's a year younger than me!"

Gratry, misunderstood prophet of the last century, inspired by God, would in turn inspire the message of John XXIII. John, who would address to the world the call of *"Pacem in Terris"* — Peace on Earth, the encyclical letter addressed to non-Christians, non-Catholics, to all men without exception. In the night of Bethlehem, didn't the celestial hosts sing a hymn of praise to God, announcing to all men "peace on earth to men with whom He is pleased."

Confronted with world politics in his role as Ambassador from the Vatican State, first to Bulgaria, in the years marked by the coming to power of Nazism and Fascism and the eruption of the most terrible of wars; then, in Paris, in the troubled post-war years, John would become convinced that the only answer to the problems that were tearing humanity apart was the message of Jesus Christ, applied and lived out on the level of nations and continents.

On April 11, 1963, the world would receive the precious gift of this document called *"Pacem in Terris"*. Frankly, without reserve, John condemns nationalism and all forms of tyranny, whether of the right or of the left. To the Christians he unveils a new field of action: "The task of putting relationships back together in human society, in truth, in justice, in love, and in freedom — bringing about real peace in God's established order."

John's letter stirs up enthusiasm, criticism, controversy. A defense in favor of man, leading to an act of faith in God, who alone can save humanity.

It is interesting, I would even say it is important, to read what they have written about him, these men who have had the privilege of meeting him, of knowing him, of discussing with him.

Bishop Fred P. Corson, of the Methodist World Council, would say: "I believe without any doubt that Pope John has instituted a religious movement which is the most significant movement in the history of the world during this century."

"From all declarations and from the example that was shown by his attitudes, it is evident that he sincerely desired to bring about a closer, more joyful unity among all Christians."

To the Methodist bishop's voice was joined that of Professor McAffee Brown, of Stanford University: "For John XXIII we were first of all brothers, and only in second place tragically separated. The extraordinary improvement in understanding and relations between Catholic and Protestant is something we would attribute largely to the initiative of John XXIII, a man who listens to the Holy Spirit. His voice, for Protestants as well as Catholics, was the voice of the good shepherd. The Catholics have lost a Pope, we have lost a friend and a brother."

"The wind blows where it wishes and you hear the sound of it, but do not know where it comes from and where it is going; so is every one who is born of the Spirit".

John 3:8

3. FRESH WIND OF RENEWAL

Who thinks "Pope John" thinks "Council". For John, the idea of a council came suddenly and unexpectedly, like all the inspirations of the Holy Spirit.

On January 25, 1959 — it was a Sunday — in the Roman basilica of "St. Paul-outside-the-Walls" John announced to the world what God had ordained to be convened: an ecumenical council.

Later, he would reveal how the Holy Spirit had spoken to his mind and heart: "Abruptly I was struck by the idea of this, within the humbleness of my spirit. The certainty that it was heaven-sent emboldened me to put my intent into action." In an unusually poetic phrase, he said the "idea sprang up within me like the first flower of an early spring."

"An ecumenical council..." in the basilica, a dramatic silence follows his words. The people have not understood. Council, ecumenical council, what is the old Pope talking about? The cardinals, the bishops, the assisting dignitaries have understood only too well, and immediately the majority disapprove. A council is a big risk in a time when so much dissent has begun to stir the deep waters on which the Roman Church is navigating.

The same evening, the Vatican press office publishes a

The papal benediction from the pontifical palace.

short stencilled paper without any heading. A brief and concise communiqué, announcing the convocation of a council by John...

Everything is there, without comment. Inside the Vatican, few are pleased with a council, and besides, there is that adjective: "ecumenical", which is so bothersome to those who insist that all dialogue is useless and sterile, from the moment that "outside the Roman church there is no possibility of salvation."

To what would be the biggest event in the history of the Roman church, radio Vatican was to consecrate exactly one minute and seventeen seconds. But, in London, the Daily Mail does over its front page in order to publish the news on seven columns. Journalists, radio reporters, television commentators leave for Rome as special permanent correspondents, while at the Vatican silence reigns.

However, everywhere in the Roman church, millions of Catholics are exulting, and the ideas — at first timidly, as on the morning after every *coup d'état* — begin to flow, for the greater glory of God. The Pope has opened a window, and inside the old buildings a wind — a rushing, mighty wind — has begun to blow.

Isn't all this an announcement of Pentecost?

It had taken twenty-five years to organize the Council of Trent. But John is in a hurry. The preparation goes slowly, one diagram after another, as illegible and incomprehensible as Parliamentary bills.

Seeing the speed with which the preparations were progressing, some feared — and obviously others hoped —

that the old Pope would die before the work began, and thus the whole thing would be postponed forever.

John wanted a meeting without barriers, *all' insegna dell' aggiornamento* — in keeping with the times. He invited brothers from all Christian churches — brothers and churches which until that day had been defined by the Roman church as "heretic", "sect" — and he wanted them as guests of honor in the first rows. John put his trust in their prayers, and in their physical presence under the vault of the old basilica of St. Peter's during the entire work of the Vatican Ecumenical Council. John knew he had adversaries in the ranks of his own church, but certainly not among the people or the clergy. His "enemies" are in high places, among those who consider the *aggiornamento* contrary to their own interests, interests often more economical and political than theological.

If the vision of Pope John XXIII is obstructed, it will be because of the hierarchy of his own church. For that reason the presence and participation of the brothers of the other Christian denominations is a source of comfort to him. Because John knows that the many Evangelicals and Lutherans, Methodists and Anglicans, Baptists and Presbyterians, Reformed and Calvinists are on his side.

For the first time in history, a Pope can have confidence in the prayers and the concrete oneness of the Christians in other denominations. John is aware of what is going on around him. He notices how others try to slow down the rhythm of the conciliary mechanism; how the council, convoked on order of the Holy Spirit to "make all things new" was being made into a festival of Vatican bureaucracy, a mystic worldly and political "happening", with speeches, parades, receptions, all on board the sinking ship that was the institutional church.

The old Pope has available a most powerful instrument, the radio. If the Vatican daily newspaper, *L'Osservatore Romano,* censors his speeches, no one will interfere when a radio message addressed to the world is transmitted live. On September 11, 1962, from his private library, John would speak to the world. Radio Vatican is linked with broadcasting stations all over the world: in Italy, France, Belgium, and in all of Latin America; while Radio Vatican itself directs its powerful revolving transmitters toward the African continent. John's is a surprise action, thanks to which the Roman Church will never be the same.

In Rome, the council fathers begin to arrive, and with them a Pentecostal prophet named David Du Plessis.

They have come for a very simple reason: they believe John's words. The Roman church wants to be renewed. The Christians of other denominations have been invited so they can see and hear. They will attend all the meetings, discussions, and encounters. The Catholic Church will confess publicly before her brothers in Christ, at last recognized as such after centuries of excommunication; she will hide nothing, she will ask for nothing except prayer, forgiveness, and understanding. This is as John wants it.

October 11, 1962, is the solemn opening day of the Council. On St. Peter's altar the Bible is in the place of honor; this gesture does not escape the notice of those brothers from other denominations. At the last minute John introduces certain changes in the program: during the celebration, the choir of the Sistine Chapel was to have sung the *"Tu es Petrus"* (You are Peter, and on this rock I shall build my church), a passage from the Gospel of

35

Matthew that for centuries has been the subject of differing interpretations. For numerous Catholics, John is Peter's successor. But for him, unity is what matters. His motto is: "Let us speak about what unites us and not what separates us." From his apartment John phones the choir director: "Take out the *'Tu es Petrus'* and sing instead that other passage of Matthew, the one that says 'Go ye and teach all nations, baptising them in the name of the Father, of the Son, and of the Holy Spirit'." These seemingly irrelevant gestures are of historical importance for those who are familiar with the churches. This gesture, too, is among those which do not escape notice, attracting the attention of journalists, the sincere joy and approbation of the masses, and, as always, the irritation of some. On that day, John would address these words to his audience, to the city of Rome, and to the entire world: "In this historical moment, Providence is leading us to a new order of human relationships, toward the realization of a superior plan."

At nightfall a huge crowd convenes on St. Peter's square, to greet John at the end of his big day. With 40,000 torches, young people form an immense cross. And once again, John will speak to those who understand him best: "Dear children, dear children, I hear your voices... One would say even the moon herself was in a hurry to come tonight. Look at the moon, my children. It is there in the sky, above us, part of this audience... My position counts for nothing; it is as a brother that I speak to you... may the Lord bless you. As you return home tonight embrace your children, and tell them it is the Pope's embrace."

From the hands of the President of the Italian Republic, Antonio Segni, John XXIII receives the Balzan International Prize for Peace, a few weeks before his death.

And this commandment we have from Him, that the one who loves God should love his brother also.

1 John 4:21

4. LOVE REACHES THE LOWEST

Such a lovely name: *Regina Coeli,* Queen of Heaven. But in Rome, when someone says *"Regina Coeli",* you think of hell, of a dark prison which centuries ago was a convent, and where the earth's damned ones live in the shadow of despair and sin. Hate, drugs, homosexuality reign between the walls of this prison, where the days and hours drop off one by one, like autumn leaves, and where words like "rehabilitation", "hope", "forgiveness", have been stricken from the vocabulary of those who have nothing left to hope for. But Jesus said: "I was a prisoner and you visited me..." The first visit John made outside the Vatican was to his brothers in *Regina Coeli.* He wanted it — and it was not easy — to be the simplest of visits. And simple were the words he addressed to these men, so far from God, yet so near to his heart. The news of his coming had spread as quickly as a tap between walls from cell to cell. And in those cells, where the prisoners lived in the most appalling promiscuity, the majority of them at first didn't want to believe. "But what's the old Pope coming here for?" Now, on that January morning, John was there in their midst, a brother among brothers, to speak to them of Christ. Of the Christ who descended into hell in order to bring a multitude of prisoners up before His Father's throne. "Brothers", says John: "It is as a brother that I come in your midst, to take your hand in mine and to see you face to face. If I were better than you it would only be by

39

grace..." That was enough to scandalise the entire Vatican court. But when John told the prisoners that as a child he went often to prison with his mother, to bring oranges to his uncle, who, as a smuggler, spent a large part of his life behind bars, this was just too much.

That evening in his private chapel, John prayed at length. The Vatican's prisoner had slipped away in order to bring to the prisoners of *Regina Coeli* a message of freedom, renewed and rediscovered freedom. With Jesus the bars do not matter; he who is in the Spirit is truly free, no matter where he happens to be. That evening, on the opposite banks of the Tiber, to John's prayers were joined the yet uncertain prayers of many of the prisoners, who, for the first time in many long years, spoke to the heavenly Father, whispering, "Forgive us our trespasses as we forgive those who trespass against us". In the sky of Rome the stars shone by the thousands. "Lord, let my brothers see this same sky."

The house where John XXIII was born, at Sotto il Monte, November 25, 1881.

John's parents:
Battista Roncalli and
Marianna Mazzola.

The three Roncalli brothers, peasants and brothers of a fourth peasant, John XXIII, proud of his origin.

Peace I leave with you; My peace I give to you; not as the world gives, do I give you. Let not your heart be troubled, nor let it be fearful.

John 14:27

5. PEACE — THE BETTER WAY

John, a man without frontiers, loved his homeland, Italy. "Love your neighbour as yourself..." How can one love humanity, the world, without first of all loving the country where one is born? At the age of twenty, like all young Italian men, John finished his military service, in 1901. Then, during the first World War, he served as chaplain in the hell of one of those Italian military hospitals so well described by Ernest Hemingway in *A Farewell to Arms*. "Military service", wrote John, "in peace and in war, was a real school for me. I learned many things about men and about life."

After the defeat at Caporetto and the turning back of the Italian army in 1917, he wrote again: "The men who governed and who are governing us do not deserve our sacrifices, but our country does deserve them. We have had our faults, but today our task is to give of ourselves to expel the Germans from Italian soil."

John, a man of peace, was conscious of the fact that sometimes the price of a battle must be paid.

John, soldier during World War I, Papal Nuncio during World War II, was the man who, under the direction of God, was able to avoid a third war which would have cost the lives of hundreds of thousands of men.

On October 22, 1962, President Kennedy addresses a message to the American nation. The U.S.S.R. has installed missile ramps in Cuba with offensive intentions toward the U.S.A. Kennedy orders a naval bloc around the island of Cuba, and the Russian boats, loaded with weaponry, will be obliged, by force if necessary, to turn back.

If the USSR reacts with an attack on Berlin, or by launching missiles from Cuban territory in the direction of the American continent, the USA will reply by attacking Soviet territory, and there will be war.

John is aware of the news which grows hourly more dramatic. In the Atlantic Ocean twenty-seven Soviet ships loaded with missiles are navigating in the direction of Cuba. Elsewhere ninety American naval units backed up by eight aircraft carriers and sixty-eight air squadrons are preparing to intercept the Soviet ships. In Florida, military units are getting ready to invade Cuba. "Since the end of World War II" — declares Adlai Stevenson, U.S. Delegate to the United Nations — "peace has never been so seriously threatened". During this time there is no contact or official dialogue between the Americans and the Soviets. But in Andover, Maryland, American writers and men of science — a small group, no more than twenty — are meeting with Russian colleagues in hope of establishing cultural ties between the two nations.

On the eve of October 23, President Kennedy telephones Andover, where his friend Norman Cousins is one of the two co-presidents of the meeting. His voice trembles: "Norman, the situation is uncontrollable. In all probability, within six hours I'll have to push the button. And that would mean one billion dead before it's over."

1914-1918. Sergeant Angelo Roncalli lives through the drama of the First World War, an experience which he will never forget...

Norman Cousins realizes that only a moral and spiritual authority, universally recognized, can save the earth from total annihilation. This authority does exist, and his name is John. In the little Maryland village, after his telephone conversation with the President of the United States, Cousins calls in a Catholic priest who is participating in the work of the convention. This man is a scholar, Father Félix Morlion, founder of the University Pro-Deo, in Rome. It is Morlion who in turn will contact John. On the other side, also at Andover are Shumko and Feodorov, Soviet scientists and personal friends of Nikita Khruschev. In their turn they recognize that only John's intervention will be able to prevent a third world war.

All during the night of October 24-25, 1962, praying, Bible in hand, John prepares a message addressed to the Soviets and to the Americans. At the first rays of dawn's light the message is delivered to the respective embassies in Rome.

The next day in Moscow, an unheard-of thing occurs: the Soviet daily *Pravda* publishes John's message on the front page, while in the Atlantic Ocean armed ships on their way to Cuba suddenly do an about-face, by order of Khruschev. A long telegram from Khruschev arrives at the White House — an offer of peace.

I do not know the text of the telegram John sent to Khruschev and to Kennedy. But I do know that in Russian the text addressed to the dictator of the Kremlin was composed of eight hundred and seventy-four words. It is expensive to send such a long telegram, but it was the price of peace, the price of over a billion human lives. It is thanks to that telegram that your children and your grandchildren are playing in the yard; it is thanks to that telegram

that there is grass in the yard. Thanks to that telegram of eight hundred and seventy-four words the Eiffel Tower, the Empire State Building, the towers of the Kremlin and the leaning tower of Pisa are still standing. God had dictated those eight hundred and seventy-four words one after another. And when a prophet speaks God's language, even unbelievers listen. "I will raise them up a prophet from among their brethren, like unto thee, and I will put my words into his mouth; he shall speak unto them all that I shall command him. And it shall come to pass that whosoever will not hearken unto my words which he shall speak in my name, I will require it of him." (Deuteronomy 18:18,19).

Khruschev understood that the Lord — the Lord of his faraway youth — was waiting at the crossroads of history. He understood that the Lord would also require it of him. And in his turn, he sent a telegram. It was much shorter; there were five or six words and it cost no more than three dollars. But thanks to this telegram the battleships turned around and there was victory for all humanity that day. For Nikita Khruschev, for John Fitzgerald Kennedy, and especially for John.

Alone with the Lord, who has heard his prayer, John prays and praises in his chapel; that day he would write in his diary a chapter from Ecclesiasticus (50: 22,23 - Jerusalem Bible):

"And now bless the God of the universe, who is doing mighty things throughout the world, who lifts up our days from our mother's womb, who acts according to His mercy to us. May He grant us a joyful heart, may He grant peace to our age, to Israel, through the centuries. May His grace rest faithfully upon us and redeem us in the time."

50

John adds: "Hallelujah, hallelujah!"

No, this time there would be no voice in Ramah of lamentations and bitter weeping; Rachel would not weep for her children.

It was not the first time that John intervened to save human lives. During the terrible Hitlerian persecution thousands of Jews owed their safety to him. During the Second World War, at Athens and at Sofia, John intervened. Certainly he did not have the prestige and renown that he would have as Pope, but even at that time he would do what he could; some cannot say as much.

Was John anti-fascist? Anti-Nazi? No. To tell the truth, John was never anti-anything; he was always pro-. In place of unfortunate ideologies he always offered an alternative ideology inspired by God. For that reason anti-communist talk was unknown to him. Not out of political calculation, but because John's thinking was essentially positive.

After his death, some made him say things he had never said nor thought. But what is certain is that John was always on the side of the humble, the downtrodden, the prisoner. John, a progressist? Don't make me laugh! Nonsense! One thing certain is that John was a man of free expression, a gift conferred on all those who, in good faith — and sometimes even by mistake — co-operate in making the church into The Church. John appears on the scene and immediately windows open: Rahner and Küng, Teilhard, Chenu and Congar, Schillebeeckx and Delubac and others come out of their secrecy.

"And a man came..." These words from the beginning

Pope John XXIII working in his garden at Castel Gandolfo.

of the Gospel of John come back to my memory like a leitmotif each time people speak about that extraordinary man, John. Extraordinary in his ordinariness, supernatural for being immersed, baptised in that spirit which is the nature of God. He didn't look down on study and research, but never missed an occasion to emphasize that Jesus, rather than calling the scholars and wise men in the academies and synagogues, had, on the contrary, turned His loving look on twelve poor sinners, crude and ignorant. He admitted them to His school and entrusted to them the task of changing humanity.

Certainly, discussions and argument resulted, but discussion is the prerogative of the living. In Antioch there was a break between Paul and Peter, and Paul was not embarrassed to call Peter a hypocrite. At times discussion is a sign of life, whereas peace reigns in the cemeteries. John, we have already said it, was not a theologian, and for that reason a new theological season sprang from his pontificate, a time of rediscovery of the Word of God.

John is a man and he wants us to remember that fact, just as Peter wanted it remembered when Cornelius tried to kneel before him. A man with limits and faults. "My position does not matter... I am your brother... and, by the way, I am not infallible!"

In 1900, in Ranica, in Northern Italy, during a strike protesting against unjust layoffs, you could see for the first time a bishop and his secretary, side by side with the workers. The bishop's name was Radini Tedeschi, and John was his secretary. In remembering Radini Tedeschi, John would write: "Some people have not yet understood, and they will understand only with difficulty that the Church and her clergymen want to love and respect all men, especially if they are Christians, and that she does not want to be subject to any political party."

John seems to be leaning to the left, but in order to restore balance let us cite a letter of praise concerning certain aspects of the dictator Mussolini's politics. At Christmas, 1939, from Istanbul, John wrote to his family in Italy, expressing his joy that his country had not yet been drawn into the war — the war already involving the Germans, the French, the British, and the Poles. "This time it really must be said: there is a hand guiding *Il Duce* in the best interests of the Italian people".

As far as politics was concerned, no one could have been more blind, and yet at the time of the last elections permitted by the Fascists in 1924, John wrote that in all good conscience he could not vote for them. "Italy's salvation cannot come from Mussolini, even if he is an intelligent man. His methods are contrary to those of the Gospel." Italy, at that time, was approaching the edge of the abyss. Violence, strikes, and crime were the order of the day. In her weakness the government did not dare interfere. There was a man who wanted to bring order, and his name was Benito Mussolini. He had on his side the war veterans, the middle class, the industrialists, the large landholders. In other words, respectable Italy, the Italy which attended mass on Sunday and was afraid of the Reds. The church endorsed Fascism, endorsed the politician she would define as "Providence's man", only to forget about him, and her reckless definition of him, the moment he and his regime fell from power.

1935. John represents the Vatican in Turkey and Greece.

For if you forgive men for their transgressions, your heavenly Father will also forgive you.

But if you do not forgive men, then your Father will not forgive your transgressions.

Matthew 6:14-16

6.   BOLDNESS AND FORGIVENESS

John is different. He will vote against *Il Duce* and will suggest to his relatives the same course of action. Because "Fascism's methods are opposed to those of the Gospel". But years later, after the victory of democracies in 1945 — when in Italy the late Mussolini seemed to have been the only member of the Fascist party — in characteristically Christian manner, John would remember the little good that Mussolini had done.

Papal Nuncio in the Balkans, John was among the first to be informed of the Germans' "evacuation politics" of persecution and extermination of the Jews. On September 5, 1940 — the war between the Allied powers and Hitler's Germany had just broken out — during a conversation with a group of Polish Jews, refugees of Wadislawi, John was told what the Germans had in store for the three million Polish Jews. That same day John contacted the Holy See by coded message. One year beforehand, on September 28, 1939, day of the German occupation of Poland, John on his own initiative had founded the committee to aid Polish refugees. In close collaboration with the Jewish agency in Jerusalem, and in agreement with Istanbul's head rabbi, Dr. Marcus, John prepared a plan to prevent the deportation of Czechoslovak and Bulgarian Jews toward the cremation ovens of Germany. In Bulgaria — Germany's ally — 25,000 innocent Hungarian Jews who had escaped from their country were to be placed

57

in the hands of the S.S. John held a tense meeting with the King of Bulgaria, Boris, assuring him in the name of Jesus an eternity in the flames of hell if he allowed these 25,000 innocent people to be placed in Hitler's hands. The meeting lasted until 3 a.m. Then King Boris gave the order to the Bulgarian police to transfer all the Jews into Turkey, a neutral country, where they were welcomed by Chaim Barbès, Jewish Agency representative in Istanbul. All during the war years, though the Church seemed to be ignoring the plight of the Jews, John would be in permanent contact with the great Palestinian rabbi Isaac Herzog. It was at the end of 1943 that a Turkish boat with 647 Jewish children on board left Istanbul for Palestine. The British government, contrary to their agreement to let Jews immigrate to the Holy land, refused to let the ship enter Palestinian waters, and the boat was directed to a German-controlled port. Rabbi Herzog contacted John, who by personal intervention — God knows how, we can truly say — succeeded in detouring the boat to a North African port controlled by the Americans. Like thousands of other Jews', these children's lives were spared thanks to John.

Several days later, the great rabbi of Jerusalem disembarked in Istanbul to embrace John and personally express to him the gratitude of the Jewish people. They had a long conversation, a conversation which, according to John, was a victory for charity, the undeniable law of life and human brotherhood.

Was John a Zionist? No. A partisan of the Jewish cause? In reality, John was on the side of all those who were unjustly wounded in body, persecuted, massacred by a diabolical system. For that reason and not by political choice John was always a friend of Israel. In Rome after his election he received an American delegation from the United Jewish Appeal. John welcomed them with these words from Psalm 4: "Answer me when I call, Oh God of my righteousness! Thou hast relieved me in my distress; be gracious to me and hear my prayer."

It is a spring full of events, the spring of 1963: the Russians launch Lunik II, an American astronaut orbits around the earth 23 times, Fidel Castro goes to Russia. In Germany, Vice-Chancellor Ludwig Ehrhard succeeds Conrad Adenauer. John receives a man who bears in his body and in his heart the suffering of the Jewish people: the father of Anna Frank, the little Jewess from Amsterdam who died in deportation and who, in her diary, had written that "in spite of everything", she continued to believe in the goodness of man.

Old Papa Frank knew that in this world there was another old man who shared his convictions, shared the same faith and hope that his little Anna had left as heritage to a humanity living in hate and resentment. He wasn't a Jew, this man; on the contrary he was the leader of a church which had for centuries relegated the Jewish people to their ghettoes, and which, with the accusation of deicide as an excuse, had allowed endless pogroms and persecutions. But this man seemed to speak a totally new language. For this reason Papa Frank had come to Rome. John, who had helped to save so many Jewish lives, was unable to hold back the tears in the presence of Anna Frank's father, and the two men embraced, weeping.

"Forgive us", whispers John. "Not only for what we have done, but for what we have failed to do." John, who had done nothing wrong, knew how and dared to make himself sin, following the example of Jesus in tak-

59

ing upon himself faults that were not his own, so that the old man facing him could do that thing most pleasing to the heart of God, that is, to forgive. The old Frank falls in the trap of love set by John, pronouncing the words that until now he has been unable to say: "Yes, I forgive. I forgive everyone..."

"Anna would be happy", thinks John, but he says nothing, sure of having said enough.

January 15, 1953. John receives his nomination and his cardinal's beret from the hands of an old socialist who has become one of his dearest friends: Vincent Auriol, President of the French Republic. "Now, with this red beret, I am more "red" than you, my dear Vincent."

Humble yourselves, therefore, under the mighty hand of God, that He may exalt you at the proper time, casting all your anxiety upon Him, because He cares for you.

1 Peter 5:6-7

7. THE HONOR OF HUMILITY

On January 1, 1945, John is named Papal Nuncio, Vatican representative to Paris. Liberated France is a deeply divided nation. During the years of the German occupation, Monsignor Valeri was the Vatican's representative to the puppet government at Vichy, presided over by the old Marshal Philippe Pétain.

Pétain had wanted to be a shield for his people, in giving — as he declared — all of himself to France. But the collaborators, traitors to the Republic, and even the Germans used the old soldier to mislead public opinion, thus creating a gap between the partisans of the Vichy government and the fighters of Charles de Gaulle's free France.

Numerous are the bishops who fall into error, dazzled by the anti-Communist crusade propagated by those who have placed themselves at the service of the Germans. John is charged with saving the situation. That same week, he goes to the office of the Minister of War, rue St. Dominique, where General de Gaulle awaits him. The General is not an easy man. At 11:00 o'clock, their agreed-upon hour, he has already drunk his seventh cup of coffee and smoked his 30th cigarette. But de Gaulle knows that free France has a debt of recognition toward the man who was also Nuncio to the Balkans and for whom free France was always the only France.

There, about to enter the War Minister's office, John meets an old friend from the time of his stay in Istanbul, Geraud Jouve, who for a time had been the French resistance's secret delegate to Turkey. Together they had worked to save a number of Jewish lives.

John shakes Charles de Gaulle's hand. "Thanks to your political foresight and energy this dear country has once again found freedom and faith in its own destiny." It is in this liberty that John will be able to resolve, one after another, the problems of the French Church, heritage of the war and of the recent past.

The months pass, months filled with happenings. On February 12, Churchill, Roosevelt, and Stalin meet at Yalta. Roosevelt dies on April 12 and Harry Truman succeeds him. The German army surrenders on May 8. August 6 and 9, two atomic bombs are exploded at Hiroshima and Nagasaki. Japan surrenders at this time.

In Paris there is a politician, a left-wing radical since the Dreyfus trial: his name is Edouard Herriot. In the past, Herriot, a confirmed anti-clerical, had strenuously fought against the economic, diplomatic, and "religious" politics of Poincaré. For a time President of the Chamber, deported to Germany by the Nazis, Herriot had become President of the National French Assembly — France's governing body. He is a priest-hater, yet strangely fascinated by Christ and by His message. It was in Paris during a meeting with John that old Herriot would meet his Lord and Savior. What exactly took place during that meeting? We will probably only know in heaven. Like the Samaritan woman at the well, Herriot may have said, "Come and see a man who told me all the things that I have done..." And certainly, just as his divine master had done, John, faced with the sincere courage of the old anti-clerical lion, would have said, "I don't condemn you". To further add — at the moment of tears and remorse — "Go, Edouard, and sin no more."

John loved France, he loved Paris. In the springtime he walked under the flowering chestnut trees on the Champs-Elysees, or along the Seine where he liked to leaf through the books sold on the stands of the Left Bank. He would pray under the arches of Notre Dame. He would drink a glass of good Beaujolais on a Pigalle terrace, go to a theatre to see Dreyer's "Joan of Arc" or Rossellini's "Saint Francis of Assisi."

France is God's land and she has felt in her own flesh the blasphemous cruelty of religious wars, during the time of the Huguenot persecution. But she is also the land of Joan of Arc, of the Curé d'Ars. In Paris a solid friendship would develop between John and Marc Boegner, President of the Reformed Church of France. They could be seen together like any pair of senior citizens, no one suspecting them of any intense activity on the terrace at Pigalle.

On January 15, 1953, John is named Cardinal and Bishop of Venice. According to an old tradition dating back to the kings of France, he would receive his nomination and his Cardinal's beret from the hands of an old socialist who had become one of his dearest friends: Vincent Auriol, President of the French Republic. "Now with this red beret, I am more red than you, my dear President." And they embrace. That same day, John says *au revoir* to Paris, leaving only friends behind, and turns his thoughts to his new destination, Venice.

Rejoice in the Lord always; again I will say, rejoice!
Let your forbearing *spirit* be known to all men. The Lord is near.
Be anxious for nothing, but in everything by prayer and supplication with thanksgiving let your requests be made known to God.
And the peace of God, which surpasses all comprehension, shall guard your hearts and your minds in Christ Jesus.

Philippians 4:4-7

8. REJOICE OVER ONE

In 1953, on arriving in Venice to take up his new position as Bishop, John found many documents on what was henceforth to be his desk: letters awaiting reply, various projects, files, piles of messages and memos, all inherited from his predecessor. John was not one of those who can make rapid-fire decisions when faced with a mountain of paper, in order to clean everything up. Since his youth he had been in the habit of examining each decision; for him to sift, to weigh, and to ponder meant to pray. And, thank God, prayer had never been difficult for him. To pray and to listen to the voice of his God — the God who never ceased speaking to his mind and heart — this was his favorite pastime.

Among the many documents his secretary wanted him to examine was one concerning a priest in trouble. "The investigation is over; it's a case with no way out. You just have to sign, your excellency, and it's all taken care of."

All taken care of. Quickly said. To sign would mean one less servant of God. One man set aside. Spiritual exile for a man who one day, certainly in good faith, had freely chosen to serve the Lord Jesus, to be a herald of His Word. Just sign here... No, John would not sign without knowing first. Besides, in the Gospel we read of the Good Shepherd who leaves His ninety-nine sheep in order to look for the one who, for some reason or other, has become lost.

The next morning very early, the *calle* — the narrow, winding streets of Venice — were deserted, and it was very early when John began his search for the lost sheep who had left his flock, the flock the Lord had entrusted to his care.

"...do you love me?" "Tend my lambs."

"...do you love me?" "Tend my sheep."

"...do you love me?" "Tend my sheep."

Arriving at the priest's home, John was greeted by an unkempt woman who did not recognize him. Of course, modern bishops, especially in Italy, are not accustomed to taking walks in the street alone at the first light of dawn.

"He's not here; he's gone out. Maybe you'll find him at the tavern, down the street."

The *bistro* was empty, at first glance, but in the shadow John soon made out the form of a solitary client, nursing a *grappa,* the Italian version of gin.

A strange meeting, that of two priests in a tavern at the hour of first mass.

"Hello, I'm glad to see you. I was looking for you."

Surprised, the man responds with a question: "Who are you?"

"I am your bishop and I'd like to talk with you."

Together they walked the distance to John's house, silently, exchanging no words. As they arrived at John's office, the silence became more and more oppressive for the lost sheep. Yes, he had sinned, he had failed to keep his word. His word that was given, not so much to men, but to God. Alcohol, women, a fraudulent administration. Now he knew that the bishop knew, and it was too late. If the bishop spoke, he knew what the verdict would be. At that moment he remembered the parable of the prodigal son who had squandered his wealth received from his father and who one day turned his steps toward home. So many times, Sundays at church after the Gospel reading, he had commented on this parable, but now it was too late for him to follow the prodigal's example. The hour of punishment was upon him.

Just then his eyes met John's, and in that look the lost sheep saw only love. Before he realized what was happening, the man who was Bishop of Venice was kneeling before him and saying, "You are a man of God, you are my brother. I want to speak to you about my sins..." After so many years, the tears began to flow and streaked the face of the unfaithful priest, tears of repentance and joy. They spoke together for a long time, putting into practice between them the teaching of James, who wrote: "Confess your sins one to another and pray for one another."

That day in the heart of this man, as in the heart of John, there was rejoicing. There was rejoicing in heaven around the throne of God, because one man was dead and lost, and had been found. He "...was dead and has begun to live, and was lost and is found." (Luke 15:32).

Let your light shine before men in such a way that they may see your good works, and glorify your Father who is in heaven.

Matthew 5:16

9. TODAY THERE IS LIGHT

'If they are willing to come, I will be happy to have them." This is what John said, and for some at the Vatican, his words were once again a cause for scandal. To receive the daughter of Nikita Khruschev, and her husband Alexei Adjubei, a Soviet journalist — it was more than a Pope should be allowed to do. Didn't they represent the elite of this atheistic Communism that the Church, by the voice of one of John's predecessors, had termed "intrinsically perverse"? And then there were the Italians, already so prone to voting Communist, who certainly would misunderstand his gesture, while the Party would know how to take advantage of it. Some tried every possible way to keep the meeting from taking place. But John chose the shortest and most logical course: that of contacting the Soviet Embassy, to whom he made it known that everyone was welcome to visit him.

John didn't forget about the church beyond the Iron Curtain, nor the suffering of Christians persecuted by Communism, but he knew that Jesus had also come for those who were farthest off.

"We must learn to distinguish" — he says to those who misunderstand his motives — "between the error and the one who errs. The Lord loves us as we are, and He died on the cross in order that His plan might be realized in the life of each human being."

71

John XXIII in his studio.

It was thus that Rada Khruscheva and Alexei crossed the threshold of the austere palace where John lived, certainly not coming as prodigal children, but only to see and know the man everyone was talking about, and in whom so many people recognized so much love. Curiosity, but also searching, and — why not? — hope.

They met a man completely different from the one they expected. In passing they brushed against the Swiss guard in multicolored uniform; the court, the pomp, the decoration were vestiges of a past which evoked museums, ancient history. But when they found themselves face to face with John they discovered in him a man living in the present and looking to the future. Certainly, John had no sympathies with Communism. On the eve of Christmas 1958, during the course of a radio message, he had said: "In several parts of the world the most sacred notions of Christian civilization have been suffocated and are extinct. The divine spiritual order has been shaken, and man's conception of supernatural life has weakened. Slavery of individuals and masses is evident in Communist countries."

To Rada and to Alexei, John made a sign to be seated. He asked if they could understand French; as they could, John was able to do without an interpreter. "I know," he said, "that usually Popes give valuable pieces of money, or books, or stamps, to queens, princesses, and ladies of high standing who come to visit them. To you, Madame, I would like to give something which has become rather rare in your country: a copy of the Gospel of Saint John." Then he continued: "I know, Madame, that you have three children. And I know their names. But I would like to hear you speak them; the names of sons, spoken by their mother, have a particular tenderness." Rada

73

Khruscheva spoke aloud the names of her three children: "Nikita, Alexei, and Ivan." "Those are very beautiful names, Madame. Nikita is not only the name of a grandfather who certainly loves his grandchildren with all his heart, but also, in our language, Niciephore, a saint of God who is very dear to me and who is buried in Venice. Alexei is Alexander, also a great saint. When I was in Bulgaria I visited a large number of sanctuaries and convents with the name of Saint Alexander. And then there is Ivan! Ivan means John, and I am John. John is the name I chose for my pontificate; it is my father's name, my grandfather's name, and the name of the hill overlooking the humble country house where I was born. For I am a peasant, madame, just like your father, and I am proud of it."

Then John addressed his words to Alexei Adjubei: "You are a journalist, and as such you must know the Bible. The Bible says that God created the world and that in one day He gave it light. The creation continued for 6 more days. But the Biblical days, as you well know, are geological eras, and these geological eras are very long. We are on the first day, my dear Alexei, my dear Rada. We are here facing each other; we see one another because there is light. Today is the first day for us, the day of *fiat-lux* — let there be light. It takes time. I say it once more: the light is in my eyes, the light is also in your eyes. The Lord will show us the way to be taken. For the moment we can only pray and believe."

When Alexei and Rada left him, John spoke to his secretary: "Maybe it will be a disappointment, but I believe there was a mysterious providential thread in all this and I don't want to break it."

The same evening in Rome, on a terrace of the Via Veneto, we dined together with Alexei Adjubei and Rada Khruscheva. We talked about international cooking, about politics, about sports. No, we did not talk about Jesus, but I felt that the memory of that extraordinary morning was present in their minds more than everything else.

"...and behold, the sower went out to sow; and as he sowed, some seeds fell beside the road, and the birds came and devoured them. And others fell upon the rocky places where they did not have much soil; and immediately they sprang up, because they had no depth of soil. But when the sun had risen, they were scorched, and because they had no root, they withered away. And others fell among the thorns, and the thorns choked them out. And others fell on good soil and yielded a crop, some a hundredfold, some sixty, and some thirty." (Mathew 13:3-8).

We do not know if the seed gave 100, or 60, or 30. Nikita Khruschev, the old grandfather who loved his grandchildren, is no longer of this world. In Moscow the rumor is whispered that he died in the grace of God: cast out by his party, but accepted by Jesus Christ, his savior.

Alexei Adjubei and Rada Khruscheva have left the Soviet capital for "destination unknown", and we know what that can mean in a country where dictatorship reigns. But surely that meeting of March 7, 1963, between two young atheists and an old believer bore and will continue to bear its fruit.

Vindicate me, O Lord, for I have walked in my integrity;
And I have trusted in the Lord without wavening.
Examine me, O Lord, and try me;
Test my mind and my heart.
For Thy lovingkindness is before my eyes,
And I have walked in Thy truth.

Psalm 26:1-3

10. THE PRICE OF INTEGRITY

Love thy neighbor as thyself... John would never have been able to love all the Christian churches, the Jews, the Moslems, and even pagans and atheists, if he had not first loved his church, the Roman and Apostolic Catholic Church, the denomination where the Lord, in His infinite wisdom, had placed him. John loved his church despite her sins, her faults, and her weaknesses. For that reason the sins, faults, and weaknesses of other churches could never diminish the love he had for them. "Jesus loves us as we are, and gave His life on Calvary so that we might become what we are called to be according to His divine plan."

"It's up to us" — John would say — "to act in such a way that the entire church of Christ might become the bride 'without spot or wrinkle... holy and blameless'."

John loved his village, Sotto-il-Monte, and his flesh-and-blood brothers in Italy, who were so near to Rome and so far from God. Concerning his country, Italy, he was waiting, like the father of the prodigal son, for her return to Christ. He never uttered a word of condemnation toward a political party. He never wanted to become involved in the battle opposing Communists and Christian Democrats. If the Communists had some aspects in common with the prodigal son, the Christian Democrats, far from being Christian and only vaguely democratic, were of the same mold as the son who stayed home without appreciating the father's gifts. Just as in the parable, the sons who stayed physically present in the father's house were scandalised when John showed evidence of his love for the lost sheep. We read in the scripture how the good shepherd left the ninety-nine sheep who were in the fold in order to seek the one who had lost its way. This was John's attitude toward the Communists. He was on the look-out, just like the father who saw his son coming from afar and who began to run to meet him. He had already prepared the white garment and the ring with the precious stone, and the fatted calf was there in the stable, waiting to be killed for the feast of reconciliation.

This is why he wrote a message to Nikita Khruschev, a severe message, yet full of love and understanding, a message that saved our civilization from what would have been the last and most terrible war. Rada Khruscheva and her husband Alexei Adjubei remembered the old man haloed with youthfulness each time they embraced their children. John had spoken to them of Nikita, Alexei, and Ivan on the day of their meeting. John had not spoken about politics, or religion, but in speaking of those children he spoke about Russia's future, the world's future.

It was more than peaceful co-existence. See how they co-exist? No, see how they love one another! In politics, co-existence is the equivalent of an *extrema-ratio* — a last resort — trying to live together only to keep from dying together in a common atomic barbecue. Everything is based on compromise, on a *modus vivendi* — a way of life — which in the long run becomes a *modus moriendi* — a way of death. To man's tolerance (in Italy the *bordellos* are called "houses of tolerance"...) John liked to oppose God's intolerance: of sin, of hate, of division between His creatures.

"That they may be one; even as Thou, Father, art in me, and I in Thee, that they may also be in us, that the world may believe that Thou didst send me, and did love them, even as Thou didst love me." (John 17:21).

On his death bed, point of take-off for real life, John repeated several times these words of Christ: "Et unum sind" — may they be one. But for John, unity did not necessarily mean uniformity, because in the Father's house are many mansions. According to the old maxim, all roads lead to Rome, but John knew that the only road leading to eternal life — "I am the way, the truth, and the life..." — does not necessarily pass through the eternal city, nor the church which has her headquarters there. All those who walk with Jesus are His traveling companions. John knew that the latter rain, just like the wind of the Holy Spirit which would soon begin to blow as it had never done before, would cause the confessional and denominational labels to come unglued. To the Bulgarians of the Orthodox Church, John addressed, at the moment of his departure from Sofia, a message of love.

For centuries, Orthodox and Roman Catholic had exchanged only excommunications and curses. In the years before the Council, John's language was unheard of. In his eyes, if the Orthodox saw themselves as sons of "another mother church", they were still sons of One Father, and at the heart of Christianity it is not mothers who matter so much as the Father. In the Gospel of Mark, it is written "...there is no one who has left houses or brothers or sisters or mother or father or children or farms, for My sake and for the Gospel's sake, but that he shall receive a hundred times as much now in the present age, houses and brothers and sisters and mothers and children and farms, along with persecutions, and in the world to come, eternal life." (Mark 10:29, 30).

John XXIII visits the tombs of the first Christians in the catacombs of Rome.

Other brothers, mothers... but no other Father, for there is one Father, and He is in heaven. Jesus said, "Do not call anyone on earth your father, for One is your Father, He who is in heaven." (Matthew 23:9).

With persecution. It is written just that way: with persecution. Persecution is the trademark of all authentic Christianity. History teaches us that when Christianity is not persecuted it becomes a persecutor. Thus John would know persecution, both during his life and after. "Blessed... when men say all kinds of evil against you falsely on account of me." Blessed John. On the eve of his death, one of his fellow-clergymen, in one of the Roman Church's highest positions, asserted that fifty years would be required just to repair the damage done by John XXIII. A cardinal who had never hidden his aversion for what he termed John's "Foolish theology" declared — behind closed doors — that the Lord, unable to open John's eyes, had finally decided to close them for good. Foolish theology? In reality it was the folly of Christ, put into action. I Corinthians 1:18 says: "For the word of the cross is to those who are perishing foolishness, but to us who are saved it is the power of God."

Yes, Christ crucified is a stumbling block, foolishness to the world, and it is still so in our day. The Lord's ways are not ours, but caught by the foolishness of Christ we begin to walk in His. Yet try, in your own surroundings, to walk in ways unlike those of others, and the least people will say of you is that you have lost your senses. Gentle and contagious madness, that of Christ who died to give us life. Gentle, wonderful madness, that of John, who at eighty-plus gives to his church a new youth, renewing his own as well.

Psalms 103:5: "Bless the Lord... who satisfies your years with good things so that your youth is renewed like the eagle's."

The teachings of scripture are valid for institutions as for individuals. A casual observer can see how true this is. Today much is said about "democratizing" the church. It is discussed in Rome, in Geneva. Unfortunately, the concrete application of the term often means making of Christ the King a constitutional monarch, conditioned by parliament. God has no intention of governing the universe with the *nihil obstat* — official seal of approval — of a senate or parliament, though it be made up of saints or angels, bishops or priests, pastors or evangelists. Actually, God is a dictator — there is only one who decides, and He is that One. Undoubtedly, God is seeking collaborators, but they are not to interfere, to decide, or even to give advice. The commandments of God, made practicable thanks to the law of love lived out in Jesus Christ — "Love one another as I have loved you" — will remain the magna carta of all humanity. Today — even in certain so-called Christian circles — discussion continues on the pros and cons of divorce, abortion, euthanasia; it is as though humanity had not long ago received God's commands. For centuries men have had difficulty putting them into practice; with sadness and remorse we have become more and more aware of our failure.

Today we have tried to simplify things, applying a law of spiritual relativity. We have declared quite simply — in the name of Jesus Christ, constitutional monarch — that what was sin yesterday or the day before is no longer sin in our day. Such a temptation never passed through the mind of John or influenced his teaching. In his encyclical letters we see nothing — word by word, line by line — but the Gospel. John was the instrument, the pen which wrote, the keyboard, the painter's brush, the sculptor's chisel, the photographer's camera, the surgeon's scalpel. Nothing more, but also nothing less.

Deprive Rembrandt of his brushes, Beethoven of his piano, Michelangelo of his chisel, and you would see them reduced to helplessness, for they could do nothing without their instruments. God also chose to impose limits on Himself and use men to serve mankind. This is why throughout history there have been Abrahams and Moses', Francis' of Assisi, Martin Luthers, with their weaknesses, their gropings, men among men and yet instruments of the divine will. This is why in the second half of our century there was John. John — instrument of a dictatorship. But if the dictatorships of men are based on discipline and obedience born of constraint and fear, the divine dictatorship is founded on a discipline and obedience born of and made real by an exchange of love between creature and Creator.

Greater love has no one than this, that one lay down his life for his friends.
You are My friends, if you do what I command you.
No longer do I call you slaves; for the slave does not know what his master is doing, but I have called you friends, for all things that I have heard from My Father I have made known to you.

John 15:13-15

11.   FRIENDS ALONG THE WAY

Many anecdotes have been told about John. To tell the truth, Pope-stories have always made the rounds in Rome, even in the past. But they were always tinted with anti-clericalism and censure. The stories told about John are true; they testify to his simplicity and Christian sense of humor.

Just like his predecessor, Pius XII, John liked to walk in the Vatican gardens. But Pius liked to walk alone, to pray and meditate, and he expressed the desire to meet no one during the course of his outings. John, on the other hand, wanted no one, including the gardener, the occasional visitor, the radio employees, to be troubled by his presence in the shadowy aisles of the *giardino*. To the police commandant, John promised not to disturb anyone. One day during his usual walk, a gardener stopped clipping shrubs to kneel down as John was passing, to ask the Pope to pray for God's blessing on himself and his family. John did so willingly. Ten minutes later, John was returning the way he had come, and once again the gardener fell on his knees asking him for the privilege of a prayer. Once again the Pope obliged him. But when John met him for the third time and the man repeated his genuflexion, John could do no less than say to him: "My dear friend, are you payed to cut shrubbery here, or to receive blessings?"

John XXIII and two of his brothers, all soldiers during World War I.

One day, on the list of participants in a special audience John had granted, he noticed a familiar name: that of a general in the Italian army, who during World War I had been his lieutenant in the military hospital of Bainsizza. Imagine the general's surprise when, upon entering John's studio, he saw the Pope saluting him with: "Sergeant Roncalli at your service...." According to the rules the old sergeant was to give homage to the officer who had been his superior in the seventy-third infantry regiment. The general was taken aback and John couldn't suppress a laugh: "You've made quite a career. When I left, you were a lieutenant and now I meet you as a general. But what do you think about mine?"

His answers were often unexpected. To an American journalist who asked him how many people worked at the Vatican, John replied, "About half of them." To a sister, Mother Superior of an order titled "of the Holy Spirit", and who had been presented to him as the "Superior of the Holy Spirit", John said, smiling, "What an honor for me, who am only the Pope and must obey the Holy Spirit's orders!"

John did not like the use of the *pluralis majestatis* — the kingly "we" which for centuries had been the prerogative of kings, popes and emperors. In fact, popes never say "I" at all, but always "we". John said "I". To Monsignor Dante, chief of Vatican protocol, who had pointed out that John should be saying "we have decided," "we thought," etc., John replied one day: "We? Why 'we'? I'm not married yet!"

April 1963. Vacation time was approaching. John asked his private physician where he planned on spending his holiday. The doctor had decided not to leave Rome be-

cause of the precarious state of John's health, and —
without revealing the real reason — told John he would
be staying in town. "Oh really?" said John. "I think you
can go ahead and enjoy the sun and the sea, because I'll
be leaving soon as well. My bags are packed, my passport
and visa are in order, and my room has been reserved
for some time now. . ."John was speaking of heaven.

Pope John XXIII blessing the participants at the Olympic Games in Rome.

The kingdom of heaven is like a treasure hidden in the field; which a man found and hid; and from joy over it he goes and sells all that he has, and buys that field.
Again, the kingdom of heaven is like a merchant seeking fine pearls,
and upon finding one pearl of great value, he went and sold all that he had, and bought it.

Mark 13:44-46

12. TRUE VALUES

John loved to entertain passing friends with a simple meal. It is around the table that new contacts are established and old ties strengthened, ties that may have been loosened by time. The simple act of eating good, plain food, prepared with care, predisposes the soul to praise the Giver of all good gifts. This was something John had learned from Jesus, who well knew the importance of sitting together at table with friends, nourishing both soul and body. It is written: "...as He was reclining at table in the house, many tax-gatherers and sinners came and joined Jesus and His disciples at the table." (Matthew 9 : 10). "And when the hour had come He reclined at table and the apostles with Him." (Luke 22 : 14). And this same Jesus said: "I grant you that you may eat and drink at My table in My kingdom..." (Luke 22 : 29).

Unlike his predecessors, who took their frugal meals in solitude, John welcomed his friends, with whom he liked to reminisce over memories of youth, spent in Sotto-il-Monte. This peaceful village was set in the neighborhood of Bergamo, and John was born there on November 25, 1881, the fourth of thirteen children. The Roncallis were certainly not rich, but *polenta* and cheese were never lacking on their table. And in the evening when the flame crackled in the old fireplace, Uncle Zaverio read aloud from Scripture, and all — John in the first row — listened to the wonderful stories of David and Goliath, Abraham and Isaac, and of Jesus, who said, "Let the children come unto me and forbid them not, for the Kingdom of heaven belongs to such as these."

Uncle Zaverio, called "the Bearded One", was the real head of the family. For a few years he had gone to primary school, making his way for miles through the snow to reach the nearest village. He had learned to read and that was all he needed. He read one book, the Bible, and cared for no other. Little John was there, listening, evening after evening.

Child, school-boy, student, priest, chaplain, diplomat, bishop, Pope — all his life John had lived, whether by accident or by choice, a life of poverty.

"Born poor," as he announced with pride, "of humble and respected folk, I am particularly happy to die poor, having contributed, according to the various needs and circumstances of my simple and modest life, to the service of the poor and of the holy Church which has nurtured me, whatever came into my hands — and it was very little — during the years of my priesthood and episcopate. Appearances of wealth have frequently disguised thorns of frustrating poverty which prevented me from giving to others as generously as I would have wished. I thank God for this grace of poverty to which I vowed fidelity in my youth, poverty of spirit, as a priest of the Sacred Heart, and material poverty, which has strengthened me in my resolve never to ask for anything — positions, money, or favors — never, either for myself or for my relations or friends."

"To my beloved family according to the flesh, from whom, moreover, I have never received any material wealth, I can

92

From his studio, linked by radio with the entire world, he makes a speech which will "straighten up" the Council.

leave only a great and special blessing, begging them to preserve that fear of God which made them always so dear and beloved to me, and to be simple and modest without ever being ashamed of it: this is their true title of nobility. I have sometimes come to their aid, as a poor man to the poor, but without lifting them out of their respected and contented poverty. I pray and will ever pray for their welfare, glad as I am to see in their new and vigorous shoots the constancy and faithfulness to the religious tradition of the parent stock, which will always be their happiness. My most heartfelt wish is that not one of my relations and connections may be missing at the final joyful reunion."

"In the hour of farewell, or better, of leave-taking, I repeat once more that what matters most in this life is: our blessed Jesus Christ, His holy Church, His Gospel, and in the Gospel above else the 'Our Father' according to the mind and heart of Jesus, and the truth and goodness of His Gospel, goodness which must be meek and kind, hard-working and patient, unconquerable and victorious."

John knew that the Lord Jesus Christ, being rich, had made Himself poor in order that we "through His poverty might become rich." (2 Corinthians 8 : 9) and that God had chosen the poor of this world to be rich in faith, inheritors of the wealth He had promised to those who love Him. Yet there was a kind of poverty that John detested and condemned: it was the poverty imposed by the selfishness of the rich, the exploitation of the masses, the work of a narrow-minded and sinful sort of capitalism. In his encyclical letter *Pacem in Terris,* John's words echoed the beatitudes: "blessed are the poor...", and also, "woe unto you who are rich, for you are receiving your comfort in full." Certainly, John was convinced that there are simple solutions for problems which appear very large, and there is supply enough in the world to meet everyone's need, but not enough for everyone's greed.

John's family was very near to his heart. He had drawn his first truths from within the bosom of his family, in his father's house during the youthful years. Noah had gone into the ark of salvation with all his family, and to his jailor Paul had announced: "Believe on the Lord Jesus Christ and you shall be saved, you and your household." (Acts 16 : 31). This was what John desired for his loved ones.

On December 1, 1961, John wrote his last letter to his family:

"I think it has been three years now since I last used a typewriter. I used to enjoy typing so much and if today I have decided to begin again, using a machine that is new and all my own, it is in order to tell you that I know I am growing old — how can I help knowing it with all the fuss that has been made about my eightieth birthday? — but I am still fit, and I continue on my way, still in good health, even if some slight disturbances make me aware that to be eighty is not the same as being sixty, or fifty. For the present at least I can continue in the service of the Lord and of the holy Church."

"This letter which I was determined to write to you, my dear Severo, contains a message for all, for Alfredo, Giuseppino, Assunta, our sister-in-law Caterina, your own dear Maria, Virginia and Angelo, and all the members of our large family; and I want it to be to all of them a message from my loving heart, still warm and youthful. Bus-

95

ied as I am, as you all know, in such an important office, with the eyes of the whole world upon me, I cannot forget the members of my dear family, to whom my thoughts turn day by day."

"My own personal serenity, which makes such an impression on people, derives from this: the obedience in which I have always lived, so that I do not desire to live longer, even a day beyond that hour in which the Angel of Death will come to call me and take me, as I trust, to paradise."

"Go on loving one another, all you Roncallis, with the new families growing up among you, and try to understand that I cannot write to all separately. Our Giuseppino was right when he said to his brother the Pope: 'Here you are, a prisoner 'de luxe'; you cannot do all you would like to do.' "

"At my death I shall not lack the praise which did so much honor to the saintly Pius X: 'He was born poor and he died poor.' "

With Robert Schuman, President of the European Assembly.

And Jesus answered and said to them, "Truly I say to you, if you have faith, and do not doubt, you shall not only do what was done to the fig tree, but even if you say to this mountain, 'Be taken up and cast into the sea', it shall happen.
And everything you ask in prayer, believing, you shall receive."

Matthew 21:21-22

13. PRAYERTIME

It was for the church the end of a long winter — a winter which had lasted for centuries. It was Spring of the year 1963; for him, for John, the last Roman Spring. And it was on the eve of that springtime that the old man with the young heart addressed a prayer to the heavenly Father, a prayer which was at the same time a message addressed to a still-frozen world.

"O Lord Jesus, you who at the beginning of your public life withdrew into the desert, we beg you to teach all men that recollection of mind which is the beginning of conversion and salvation."

"Leaving your home at Nazareth and your sweet Mother, you wished to experience solitude, weariness, and hunger. To the tempter who proposed to you the trial of miracles, you replied with the strength of eternal wisdom, in itself a miracle of heavenly grace."

"It is Lent."

"O Lord, do not let us turn to 'broken cisterns' that can hold no water (Jer. 2 : 13) nor let us be so blinded by the enjoyment of the good things of earth that our hearts become insensible to the cry of the poor, of the sick, of orphan children and of those innumerable brothers of ours who still lack the necessary minimum to eat, to clothe their nakedness and to gather their family together under one roof.''

"You also, Jesus, were immersed in the river of Jordan, under the eyes of the crowd, although very few then were able to recognize you; and this mystery of tardy faith, or of indifference, prolonged through the centuries, is a source of grief for those who love you and have received the mission of making you known in the world.''

"O grant to the successors of your apostles and disciples and to all who call themselves after your Name and your Cross, to press on with the work of spreading the Gospel and bear witness to it in prayer, suffering and loving obedience to your will!''

"And since you, an innocent lamb, came before John in the attitude of a sinner, so draw us also to the waters of the Jordan. To the Jordan will we go to confess our sins and cleanse our souls. And as the skies opened to announce the voice of your Father, expressing His pleasure in you, so, having successfully overcome our trial and lived austerely through the forty days of our Lent, may we, O Jesus, when the day of our Resurrection dawns, hear once more in our innermost hearts the same Father's voice, recognizing us as His children.''

In this message speaking of the desert, of the cross, and of the resurrection there was also a reflection of John, of that solitude which is characteristic of those who are never alone because they live in the light of the Lord. The prophet Isaiah had announced that "The wilderness and the desert will be glad, and the Arabah (desert) will rejoice and blossom like the crocus. It will blossom profusely, and rejoice with rejoicing and shouts of joy. The glory of Lebanon will be given to it, the majesty of Carmel and Sharon. They will see the glory of the Lord, the majesty of our God. Encourage the exhausted, and strengthen the feeble. Say to those with palpitating heart, take courage, fear not. Behold, your God will come with vengeance, the recompense of God will come, but He will save you." (Isaiah 35 : 1-4).

The world seemed still to be desert on the eve of this new springtime. But that desert could prove to be a mirage... "the scorched land will become a pool, and the thirsty ground springs of water; in the haunt of jackals, its resting grass becomes reeds and rushes. And a highway will be there, a roadway and it will be called the 'highway of holiness'." (Isaiah 35 : 7-8)) Yes, without a doubt, spring was in the air.

And when the day of Pentecost had come, they were all together in one place.

And suddenly there came from heaven a noise like a violent, rushing wind, and it filled the whole house where they were sitting.

And there appeared to them tongues as of fire distributing themselves, and they rested on each one of them.

And they were all filled with the Holy Spirit and began to speak with other tongues, as the Spirit was giving them utterance.

Acts 2:1-4

14. PENTECOST

"On the point of presenting myself before the Lord, One and Three, who created me, redeemed me, chose me to be priest and bishop and bestowed infinite graces upon me, I entrust my poor soul to His mercy. Humbly I beg His pardon for my sins and failings: I offer Him what little good, even if imperfect and unworthy, I was able with His help to do, for His glory and in the service of the Holy Church and for the edification of my fellows, and I implore Him to welcome me, like a kind and tender father, among His saints in the bliss of eternity."

"Like a kind and tender father...". In the pages of John's will we find expressed so clearly what had always been his relationship with God. This is the conscientious report of the son who knows he can confide everything, ask anything of his loving father. John loved to cite the passage of Psalms 103 : 11-13:

"For as high as the heavens are above the earth, so great is His lovingkindness toward those who fear Him."

"As far as the east is from the west, so far has He removed our transgressions from us."

"Just as a father has compassion on his children, so the Lord has compassion on those who fear him."

On a visit to the Italian city of Loreto, John thanks the machinists on the train taking him to his destination.

"Wisdom is there, and only there, in the divine book, the Bible," John used to say.

All across Italy, nuns were scattering to sell the Bible from house to house. In three months the Italians had bought more Bibles than in the entire three centuries preceding John's pontificate.

"You don't give away the Bible. You sell it. You can sell it at a complete loss, but the fact of having paid for it invites people to read it."

John, who had placed the Bible in plain sight, in the place of honor on St. Peter's altar, the day of the Council's opening, wanted it to have a special place in each home as well.

The days passed, the weeks, the months. John's health weakened. But John was not afraid. He wrote one day: "I feel that Jesus is drawing nearer and nearer to me. During these days he has allowed me to plunge into the depths and be submerged in the realization of my wretchedness and pride, to show me my urgent need of him. When I am about to sink, Jesus, my Savior, comes smiling towards me, walking on the waters. I would say to Him with Peter: "Depart from me, for I am a sinful man, O Lord." but I am prevented by His tender heart, and His kind voice saying: 'Do not be afraid.' I fear nothing more when I am with you. I rest on your bosom, like the lost sheep; I hear the beating of your heart. Jesus, I am yours once more, forever yours. With you I am truly great; a fragile reed without you, a column of strength when I lean on you. I must never forget my own helplessness and so shall always distrust myself. Even when I am bewildered and humiliated I must always cling most trustfully to you, because my helplessness is the seat of your mercy and your love. Good Jesus, I am always with you, never go away from me."

On March 1, an international commission made up of Americans, Russians, French, Italians, Germans, and Swiss conferred upon John the International Balzan Peace Prize. On May 22, eve of Ascension, his doctors forbade him to go to St. Peter's, where hundreds of believers were waiting for him. There were, among others there, French and Chinese (from the U.S.A., the entire crew of the aircraft carrier Shangri-La). From the window of his private library he would speak to the crowd jamming the square. "Today is the day celebrating the ascension to heaven of our Lord Jesus Christ. Who among us wouldn't want to follow Jesus, being lifted up into eternal glory? But for those who stay here on earth, the most natural commitment for each Christian is to imitate the apostles who met in the upper room, praying for the Holy Spirit to descend."

Then came Pentecost. As John was preparing to leave this world a huge crowd — 400,000 people — kept watch out on the public square, day and night, in prayer. The doctors attending to John thought he would die at any moment on that festival day. But Pentecost is not for dying, Pentecost is a festival of life, of new birth.

Then came Pentecost Monday. In John's room his secretary was celebrating the Eucharist and reading the passages of scripture which tell of the day that saw the birth of the church: "And when the day of Pentecost had come, they were all together in one place. And suddenly there came from heaven a noise like a violent, rushing wind, and it filled the whole house where they were sit-

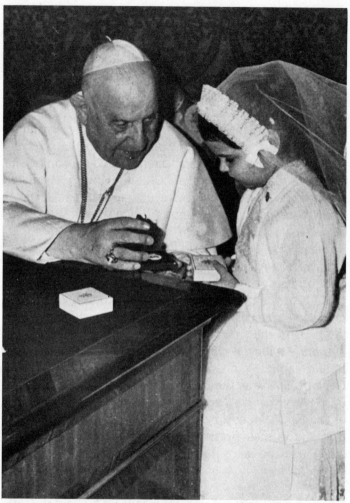

Ill with leukemia, she came from America to Rome for her first communion. John XXIII prays for her healing.

ting. And there appeared to them tongues as of fire distributing themselves, and they rested on each one of them. And they were all filled with the Holy Spirit and began to speak with other tongues as the Spirit was giving them utterance." (Acts 2 : 1-4).

John had lost consciousness hours previously. But suddenly his voice rang out. He called his secretary by name: "Loris, read that passage once more." In the Catholic Church for centuries all had been regulated chronometrically; according to the calendar-bound liturgy the same passage couldn't be read twice. If you wanted to hear it again you had to wait until the next year. But John respected God's laws much more than rules established by men. Ready to enter into eternal glory, he lived his last moments on earth as he had always lived — in the freedom of a son of God. In his room on the fifth floor he could hear the murmuring of prayers mounting from the public square. His friends were there, his true friends — the poor in the first row. They had come from faraway *borgata* — slums — the Communist belt surrounding the Italian capital: Gordiani, Quarticciolo, Quinto Miglio, Labaro. This was the crowd that usually came to Rome once every year on May first, Labor Day — to form a sea of red flags. Now they were there with prayers on their lips, and in their hearts the chagrin at seeing a dear one die. These too were lost sheep, at last recognizing their shepherd.

At seven p.m. that evening John gave up his soul to God, the soul that had always belonged to Him. A window, the one on John's room, lit up, and the crowd understood that John was living forever.

It was at that moment that a white dove descended from a

sky blazing with the reflection of sunset, brushed over the heads of the crowd, and circled the obelisk in the center of St. Peter's square. The silence was so complete that the flapping of his wings could be heard. Three times around the obelisk: in the name of the Father, of the Son, and of the Holy Spirit.

It was like that dove which came down the day heaven opened, when Jesus went into the waters of Jordan and the Father's voice resounded from on high to announce to all men, "This is my beloved Son..."

It was the end of a day, that Pentecost Monday in 1963. It was the eve of a brand-new day.

In Rome, there is a wind which blows each evening at dusk, at nightfall — this wind is called *il Ponentino* — the West Wind. That evening, the wind, always gentle, became violent, like the wind on the long ago day of Pentecost. "Come from the four winds, O breath, breathe on these slain, that they come to life." (Ezekiel 37 : 9).

The sky, far from darkening and sparkling with stars, became red — more and more red. Red as the tongues of fire that, from this same sky, came down on the disciples gathered in the upper room. In answer to John's prayer, the Lord was preparing to renew, on a scale thousands of times greater, the miracles of the first Pentecost.

And Jesus came up and spoke to them, saying, "All authority has been given to Me in heaven and on earth. Go therefore and make disciples of all the nations, baptizing them in the name of the Father and the Son and the Holy Spirit,
teaching them to observe all that I commanded you; and look, I am with you always, even to the end of the age."

Matthew 28:18-20

15. GOING ON

I have met some uncommon men in the course of my life; that is part of my profession as a journalist. Men of science, such as Werner von Braun and Albert Einstein. Von Braun, despite his American passport, was a German whose youth was marked by the Swastika and who, after the "twilight of the gods" — and maybe as a result of looking so often toward heaven — had at last discovered that infinite space is God's domain, not the domain of V1's, V2's, and interplanetary missiles.

Once with Albert Einstein, in the fifties, I had a long chat on the terrace of an Italian airport, surrounded by fog. "In our day there is fog everywhere; our planet seems to be aimlessly drifting — deprived of its spiritual radar. And yet, beyond that grayness the sun is shining. Someone will have to take us by the hand and lead us to the light...". In the old man's tone, a mixture of disappointment and hope.

I have met politicians, like Robert Schuman, the father of a Europe whose birth pains are being felt. Like Conrad Adenauer, a stubborn believer who sprang up in 1945 at retirement age, from among the debris of a Germany lying in ruins — to die standing up, after having completed his work of reconstruction.

And I think yet of other men I have met: of Charles de

December, 1959. U.S. President Eisenhower laughs heartily at some witty remark by Pope John XXIII during the December 6 Vatican audience. The Pope speaks to Ike in the, for him, unfamiliar English language. Also seen in the photo is Mrs. Barbara Eisenhower, Ike's daughter-in-law, and interpreter Lt. Colonel Vernon Walter.

Gaulle, that hard-headed Fleming, as sure of France's greatness and of the God of the French as he was sure of his own personal greatness. Of Haile Selassie, emperor of Ethiopia and direct descendant of Solomon and the Queen of Sheba, who — rare virtue for a statesman — knew how to forgive the trespasses of those who had trespassed against him. And yet again: of De Gasperi, a man of action and of prayer as Italians can, but seldom will, be. Of Dwight Eisenhower, liberator of at least 500 European cities and towns whose names he couldn't pronounce; of John Kennedy, prince charming, prisoner of his "new frontiers". And the list could go on.

Then I met John, and I can assure you that he was altogether different. Convinced that no one is born righteous, conscious that alone he could do nothing and at the same time sure that he could do "all things through Him who strengthens..." (Philippians 4 : 13). All his life he had been able to grow in grace; as in Psalm 131, he had neither a "proud heart", nor "haughty eyes", but a "composed and quiet soul". Like a "weaned child who rests against his mother", he had put his hope in the Lord. The "great matters and things too difficult" for him as a creature, he had simply put in the hands of his Creator. From the day he made himself a servant of God, August 10, 1904, he had chosen God as the North Star of his existence, hoisting high his soul's sail to capture the wind of the Spirit, entrusting the helm to the divine navigator, Jesus Christ.

John, the misunderstood. Today when people speak of him I have the impression they are speaking of another man and not the one I have known. He is described at times as a joyful man. True, he had joy, having accepted the free gift of joyful and abundant life. But the refusal of

113

so many others, offered this same gift, was like a "sword piercing his own soul."

With David in Psalm 126, John could say that the Lord had done great things for him and that he was glad. And in time of sorrow he could declare with certainty that "those who sow in tears shall reap with joyful shouting; he who goes to and fro weeping, carrying his bag of seed, shall indeed come again with a shout of joy, bringing his sheaves with him."

"Lord, renew in your church the miracles of a new Pentecost..." John had sown with tears. But if, on the evening of the Council's opening, he was able to say to the crowd that never in its history had the old basilica of Saint Peter's seen such a spectacle — 13 years later, in that same church, the spectacle of thousands and thousands of Catholics, baptized in the Spirit of Pentecost, was still more striking. It was the divine reply to his prayer.

A new Pentecost. This is what John had asked of the Lord his God. "All things for which you pray and ask, believe that you have received them, and they shall be granted you." (Mark 11 : 24). For the first time in history, Catholics, born again and baptized in the power of the Spirit of God, came to St. Peter's, not to receive but to share the gifts they had received from heaven, in order that these might become the heritage of the entire church. In St. Peter's on that day, maybe for the first time, the voice of the Lord would speak through prophecy:

"Because I love you I want to show you what I am doing throughout the world."

"I am preparing you for what is coming."

"Days of shadows are coming on the world, days of tribulation... Buildings which are standing will stand no more. The things which are supporting my people now will no longer be there."

"I wanted you to be prepared, my people, to know only me... to lean on me and possess me in a deeper way than ever before."

"I will lead you into the desert. I will deprive you of everything you now depend on, so that you only depend on me."

"A time of darkness will come on the world, but a time of glory will come for my church, for my people."

"I will pour out on you the gifts of my Spirit."

"I will prepare you for a spiritual combat; I will prepare you for a time of evangelism as the world has never seen..."

"And when you have nothing left but me, you will have everything: lands, fields, houses, brothers, sisters, love and peace and joy more than ever before."

"Be ready, my people, I want to prepare you."

That joyful day was a Pentecost Monday. In the crowd were Catholics and Pentecostals, Methodists and Baptists, Anglicans and Orthodox — representatives of the churches that John liked to call sister churches, daughters of one Father, all participating in the celebration. The

115

language of heaven had replaced the Latin of our ancestors, and John's successor greeted the crowd by pro-
claiming: "Jesus is Lord, hallelujah! hallelujah!"

That day the song of h-a-l-l-e-l-u-j-a-h rose up toward the
clear sky of Rome; on high, the angels and saints joined
the song of God's people on earth.

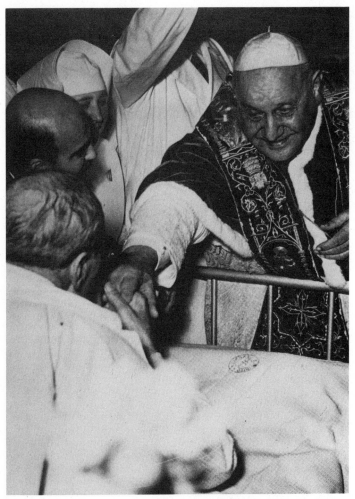

In a Roman hospital, John XXIII visits the poorest sick people.

And He said to them, "Go into all the world and preach the gospel to all creation.

He who has believed and has been baptized shall be saved; but he who has disbelieved shall be condemned.

And these signs will accompany those who have believed: in My name they will cast out demons, they will speak with new tongues;

They will pick up serpents, and if they drink any deadly poison, it shall not hurt them; they will lay hands on the sick, and they will recover."

Mark 16:15-18

16. ALL TOGETHER

And now? What will happen now that John is no longer with us? In the old Roman Church, many things are changed. Here and there. A church fed on Bibles is being raised up in place of the church-power. In his opening speech of the Vatican Council, on October 11, 1962, John had cited these words of Christ: "Now learn the parable of the fig tree: when its branch is tender and puts forth its leaves, you know that summer is near; even so, you too, when you see all these things, recognize that He is near, right at the door." (Matthew 24 : 32-33). John had also said: "The Kingdom of Jesus Christ is completely at the service of humanity, but it is not subject to what is material, exterior, and transitory in religion. Jesus of Nazareth fixed the fundamental lines of the ecclesiastical organizations but he did not connect them to locality or circumstance. The tempest blows and shakes the most solid buildings, devastating and transforming everything. But this is of no importance. Everything here is passing away; everything must be renewed, like clothes that wear out, become threadbare."

One thing is certain: John (who insisted that the church's leader was not the Pope, but Jesus Christ) had placed the Roman Catholic Church — which wisdom, one might say the cleverness of the Holy Spirit, had entrusted to him — in the hands of the One who is the chief cornerstone of the church, and the only mediator between man and God, Jesus Christ. (1 Timothy 2 : 5). Thus after her *periodo Giovanneo* the church will never be the same. She will not become the Church, so desired by the conservatives, wanting to stop the clocks and calendars, nor will she become the extremist church dreamed of by the progressists, who envision a mini-god reduced to human dimensions.

We have learned some things during these last few years; years which are — which we now live in — the time preceding the return of our Lord. In the Roman Catholic Church we have learned to know, to appreciate, and to love brothers in Christ, coming from the purifying bath of the Reformation as jealous guardians of the Word of God. Our Orthodox brothers, who for centuries have kept alive the worship in the Holy Spirit, and the Pentecostals, who confirm by their experience what John had foreseen and desired: the realisation of Joel's prophecy. "And it shall come about after this that I will pour my Spirit on all mankind; and your sons and daughters will prophesy, your old men will dream dreams and your young men will see visions. And even on the male and female servants will I pour out My Spirit in those days." (Joel 2 : 28).

Let us seek to understand one another, to discover what unites us. It is in understanding one another that we will be able to love one another.

For centuries Roman Catholics have been steeped in the teaching of *extra-ecclesia nulla salus* — outside the Church is no salvation — and for Catholics this meant the Roman Catholic Apostolic Church. For the Protestants the Church of Rome was the woman of Revelation 17 : 15. "...the waters which you saw where the harlot sits are peoples and multitudes and nations and tongues." — and this was probably the only point on which they were in agreement among themselves. For the Pentecostals and their numerous "infallible popes" the watchword was "no salvation outside of Pentecostalism." Thank God, all this is changing and this *metanoia,* this transformation, makes us more believable to the world.

Franz Konig, a cardinal of the Roman Church and archbishop of Vienna, said on September 12, 1974 in Rome: "The church of the future will be more honest and more modest. She will profess her faith in simplicity. In the future there will be a religion of freedom, not limiting the personal space and individual characteristics of men. Because where the Spirit of the Lord is, there is liberty. The religion of the future will be open to the human condition. Better than we do today she will know how to discern the essential from the accidental. Better than in the past, the church of the future will be conscious of her prophetic mission. For the world, prophets are troublesome; they are sometimes troublesome for the church. The church of the future will find herself in difficulty with the powers of this world, but she will not let her voice be silenced by money or by privilege, just as she will not be brought down to the level of political systems. The church of the future will not be the church of imposing organisations or large display. She will be carried, supported by little communities. We are at the end of the time of great, empty organisations; the movement, the life of the church is in the small groups."

Divisions at the heart of the different churches prevent in turn unity between the churches, the *unum sint* between all the denominations; a precious mosaic that should make the body of Christ visible to unbelievers. No group,

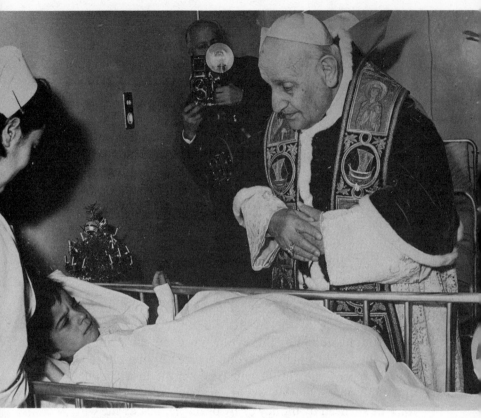

A prayer for a sick child, in the hospital Bambin Gesù.

no church, no believer holds absolute monopoly on the truth, except Jesus Christ, He who is the "way, the truth, and the life." But there are parts of the truth in each group, church, and trend that confesses Jesus Christ as savior and Lord.

Personally, I believe that, more than ever in our time, to live our faith means to put into practice, as a Christian redeemed by Christ's sacrifice, born again and baptized in the Holy Spirit, the three essential tasks of each believer, each Christian community. These tasks are the proclamation of the Gospel of our Lord Jesus Christ, the *kerygma* — testimony — which may go as far as martyrdom (our persecuted brothers are proof of that — *martyrion)* and finally, service — *diakonia* — of our fellowmen, as creatures of the same God, whether or not they are conscious of Him.

Jesus said, "For if they do these things in the green tree, what will happen in the dry?" (Luke 23 : 31).

John was criticized by some who had attained the highest echelons of his church, which he loved unreservedly, all the while equally loving all those who called themselves Christ's. Some called him "the Good Pope", saying that he was too good. As though goodness, fed by supernatural love, were not the forgotten element whose absence makes our society empty, sterile, and cold. But for those thousands and thousands men and women, and first and foremost for those who are "poor in spirit, who weep, who are gentle, those who hunger and thirst for righteousness, the merciful, the pure in heart, the peacemakers, those who are persecuted for righteousness' sake, for those whom men insult, persecute, and against whom they say all manner of evil falsely", for them John, the beloved, was a brother, a brother who loved unconditionally. And after having told his story, I only wish to add: "Go thou, and do likewise."

The Archbishop of Canterbury, Dr. Donald Coggan, praying before the tomb of John XXIII.

EPILOG

YOU, TOO, CAN BE INVOLVED

Many years have passed. Pope Pius XII spoke of an imminent, new springtime, and it was whispered around him that he was a visionary, a dreamer. Those who said so were unaware that they were emphasizing the words of the prophet Joel: "In the last days... old men shall dream dreams..."

John XXIII, God's sentinel, had seen beyond the horizon at a time when the darkness seemed heavy, to the dawning of a new day, for the church and for the entire world.

"My soul", he had said, "is resting in the hope of a new Pentecost in which will be re-established the victory of truth."

The charismatic Renewal is not a search for what is new, but a return to the source, a turning back to Him who is the Chief Cornerstone.

Thanks to John XXIII, following in his steps, we have discovered and explored the ancient and eternal truths, and this exploration is far from being complete. I am reminded of certain verses of T. S. Eliot: "We shall not cease from exploration, and the end of all our exploring will be to arrive where we started, and know the place for the first time."

It all began at Pentecost, and is beginning there again. Together for the first time as Christians of all denominations, we have sought entry to the upper room, to discover there a door that we thought closed centuries ago, which was always open to us.

How could I help but thank God for His men, men I have met along my way, and who, each in his own way, revealed to me some hidden truth. I think of Frank Buchman, a son of Pennsylvania, citizen of the world, a man listening attentively to the Holy Spirit, who revealed to me that God speaks, and never stops speaking, to those who listen.

I think of John XXIII, for whom Pentecost was a joyous, living reality.

I think of Father Werenfried van Straaten, God's beggar and defender of ancient truths, who, in the face of injustice and persecution, was able to unleash a wave of generosity and love unknown in history.

I think of Father Valérien Gaudet, hardened seeker after the things of God, an old Canadian chiseled in wood, who knocked at my door one night to introduce me to the charismatic renewal.

I think of Billy Graham, the great Baptist preacher, who, in Rome, was able to answer my questions by telling me simply that the Holy Spirit would guide me into all truth.

I think of Pastor John McTernan, who was for me teacher, father, and brother, and who after my baptism in the Spirit of God, led me by the hand through the pages of Scripture, always emphasizing — good Pentecostal that he was — that my place was in that old Roman Catholic Church, where the will of God had put me.

And then I think of Demos Shakarian, who invited me, years ago, to work with him and thousands of other brothers in this last world-wide revival preceding the return of our Lord Jesus.

What an extraordinary era we have the privilege of living in. I recently met in Rome with Pope John-Paul II, that unhoped-for pontiff whom Billy Graham called the "moral leader of the world". I presented him with the story of Demos Shakarian and the men of his Fellowship, the F.G.B.M.F.I., the Full Gospel Business Men's Fellowship.

In the U.S.A., on a television interview with Demos Shakarian, I was a guest on the program "Good News", and, questioned about John XXIII by him, I answered, "It is in you, Demos, that I find that same enthusiasm, the same spirit of prophecy, the same discernment which is the wisdom of the simple, which I have seen in John XXIII." I saw Demos' eyes fill with tears.

But let me tell you about Demos Shakarian: the voice of God spoke to him in 1952, that same voice which had spoken before to John XXIII, and which, thanks to their obedience, had made of these two men — so different, and yet so near to one another — precursors of what was to come.

"I, and I alone, Demos, can open doors. I take away the beams from the eyes of men who no longer see. And now I will enable you to see the truth." And then Demos saw millions and millions of men, their faces set, lifeless and miserable. Though near one another, shoulder to shoulder, they had no contact with each other. They stared, wide-eyed, but saw nothing. Faces like brass, faces black or white, all were equally hard, without feeling, and each one of them was imprisoned in his own death. Then the voice of the Lord rang out again, saying: "What you now see is going to happen very soon." Demos Shakarian saw millions and millions of men, but what a difference! All heads were raised, their eyes shone with joy, their hands were raised to heaven, worshipping. All these men who had been alone, prisoners of self, were now linked together in a community of love and prayer. In Asia, in America, in Europe, in Africa, everywhere, death was changed into life.

Yes, prophets confirm the prophets, as the Scripture teaches us. Frank Buchman had spoken of a coming revolution, the last one, through which the cross of Christ would transform the world. Pius XII had proclaimed a new springtime. The vision of John XXIII had newly underlined the task that God gave to those He loves, which is to repair relationships, bringing truth, justice, love, and freedom into the world, bringing about peace through God-given order, as he said in his encyclical, *"Pacem in Terris"*.

The extraordinary merit of Demos Shakarian is to have been able to set up spiritual platforms, where Christians, filled with the Spirit of Pentecost, meet together, freed by the bonds of a unity going beyond uniformity, transforming the destiny of men and nations according to the plan of God. The F.G.B.M.F.I. is not a new church, but an arm of the church of Christ, men of every continent revealing to the world the power of the Resurrected One and the love of their Saviour, witnessing in season and out of season to what the Lord has done in their lives. You too, can be involved today.

I know what I am talking about when I say that through the charismatic renewal, as through these men of the F.G.B.M.F.I. — men who have accepted everything God has to give, by His Holy Spirit, in order to be able to give in their turn — through these, the vision of a new Pentecost, as seen by John XXIII, is being made reality. It is a reality perhaps beyond our expectations, but certainly not beyond his.

INDEX OF NAMES

Ioannes P. P. XXIII